CANTICLES
in
CANDLELIGHT
A CANTATA FOR CHRISTMAS

Joseph M. Martin

Full Orchestration by Brant Adams
Chamber Orchestration by Stan Pethel

Performance time: Approx. 45 Minutes

(1) This symbol indicates a track number on
the StudioTrax CD or SplitTrax CD.

ISBN 978-1-4803-8518-4

SHAWNEE PRESS

EXCLUSIVELY DISTRIBUTED BY

HAL•LEONARD®
CORPORATION

7777 W. BLUEMOUND RD. P.O. BOX 13819 MILWAUKEE, WI 53213

Visit Shawnee Press Online at
www.shawneepress.com

FOREWORD

In faithful succession, the sacred flames of Advent's candles shine against winter's cold gray shadows with an unrelenting message of hope, peace, love and joy. Against a seemingly endless night, the candles gleam with sparkling promise. "A Light shines in the darkness, yet the darkness has not overcome it."

With great expectation, we gather close to the flickering flames and gather strength for our journey to dawn. We warm our spirits at the hearth of worship. We linger in the glow of prayer and devotion and discover the illumination of truth and the warmth of fellowship.

As we gaze into the dancing gold we discover a deeper truth; we are the candles! We are a light on a hill and a beacon of hope, peace, love and joy in the night. We are torches of truth, ignited by grace and refined by fire. As we are consumed, we shine forth the glory of God! Animated by winds of the Spirit we give ourselves to the miracle of the message; "Jesus, the Light of the World has come and we are His children of Light."

Joseph M. Martin

Scriptures used in the narrations are from Isaiah 9:2, 40:1-3, 49:6b, 52:7,10, 60:1-3; Jeremiah 29:11; Matthew 1:18-23, 2:1-2,10-11, 5:15-16; Luke 1:26-33, 2:8-15; John 12:36; Ephesians 5:8.

PROGRAM NOTES

Canticles in Candlelight uses music, scripture, narration and the lighting of candles to convey the story of Jesus' birth. The "Prologue" establishes a reflective spirit of worship for the opening of the work before the entrance of the singers. It is recommended that this overture be played in darkness as much as is possible. Following the "Prologue," a narrator, holding a single lighted candle speaks the opening scripture, "The Light shines in the darkness, and the darkness has not overcome it." *(John 1:5)*

For the "Processional of Lights," it is recommended that between every few singers, an accompanying non-singing acolyte processes, thus creating a gentle, illuminated path through the darkness. This opening piece can be sung as notated, or the parts can be evenly divided among the singers to create vocal balance as the choir enters from various places in the sanctuary. As the choir reaches its place in the loft the acolyte's candles are then scattered across the front of the worship space in pleasing balance. The stage is now set for the rest of the work.

With each movement of the cantata a special candle is illuminated during or immediately following each reading. Different colored candles, or banners may be used to bring attention to these worship symbols. These may be placed on the altar or in special holders to set them apart from the candles that were put in place by the acolytes. These candles represent prophecy, hope, peace, joy, love, the Christ candle, adoration and worship, and faith.

There are two possible endings for this cantata. One, is a festive hymn montage with the option of congregational participation. The other features a contemplative epilogue ending with the choir surrounding the auditorium and "passing of the light" to everyone as "Silent Night" is sung.

SCRIPTURE FOR CONTEMPLATION

And those who are wise shall glisten like the brightness of the sky above; and those who turn many to righteousness, will shine like the stars forever and ever. *(Daniel 12:3)*

*This cantata is dedicated to James Barnard in gratitude
for his enduring friendship and dedicated work.
May all of your life be filled with beautiful music.*

PROLOGUE

Tune: **VENI EMMANUEL**
Plainsong melody
Arranged by
JOSEPH M. MARTIN (BMI)

NARRATION:
The Light shines in the darkness, and the darkness has not overcome it.

PROCESSIONAL

Words:
Latin Hymn
tr. JOHN MASON NEALE (1818-1866)
Liturgy of St. James, 5th Century
tr. GERARD MOULTRIE (1829-1885)

Tunes:
VENI EMMANUEL
Plainsong melody
PICARDY
Traditional French Carol
Arranged by
JOSEPH M. MARTIN (BMI)

8

Christ our God to earth de - scend - ing,

our full hom - age to de - mand.

SOPRANO

ALTO

BARITONE

Re - joice! Re - joice! Em - man - u - el shall

10

come to you, O Is - ra - el! Re -

joice! Re - joice! Em - man - u -

el shall come to you, O Is - ra -

CANTICLES IN CANDLELIGHT - SAB

NARRATION:

Hear this word from the prophet Isaiah:

The people walking in darkness have seen a great light. On those living in the land of deep shadows, a light has dawned.

Comfort, comfort my people, says your God. Speak tenderly to Jerusalem; and proclaim to her that her struggles are at an end. Her sins have been redeemed; and the Lord's hand has poured out grace upon her sins. Listen! There is a new voice calling in the wilderness, "Prepare the way of the Lord, make straight in the desert a highway for your God."

(Light the candle of Prophecy.)

PREPARE AND CELEBRATE

Words and music by
JOSEPH M. MARTIN (BMI)
Incorporating tune: **SCHULZ**
by JOHANN A. P. SCHULZ (1747-1800)

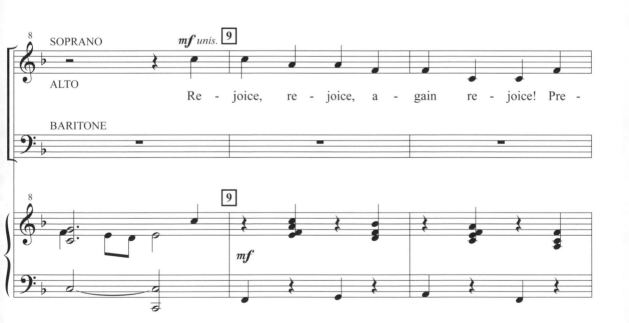

14

pare the way.

Pre - pare the way.

SOPRANO

ALTO

O come all you peo - ple and

wel - come the Light. A star out of

* Tune: SCHULZ, Johann A. P. Schulz, 1747-1800

CANTICLES IN CANDLELIGHT - SAB

Ja - cob will shine in the night. Fling

BARITONE

o - pen the doors of your heart, and re -

joice! Pre - pare ye the way with your

20

lives____ and your voice. Pre - pare ye the

way. Sing a joy - ful noise, joy - ful noise.

joy - ful noise, joy - ful

Lift a joy - ful noise un - to - the Lord_____

noise, joy - ful noise un - to the Lord._____

cresc. poco a poco

pare ye the way of the Lord. Make ev - 'ry

pare ye the way of the Lord.

high - way straight. Soon we will cel - e - brate!

unis.

Al - le - lu - ia! Sing to the Lord! Sing to the Lord!

NARRATION:

Hear these words of assurance from Jeremiah:

For I know the plans I have for you, says the Lord, they are plans for good and not for evil. I am giving you a future filled with promise and hope.

(Light the advent candle of Hope.)

ADVENT LONGING

Words by
JOSEPH M. MARTIN (BMI)
Quoting: "Savior of the Nations, Come"

Music by
JOSEPH M. MARTIN (BMI)
Incorporating tune:
NUN KOMM, DER HEIDEN HEILAND

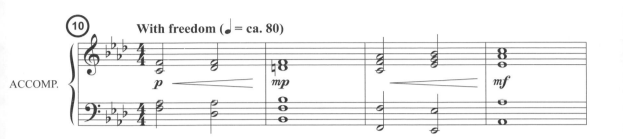

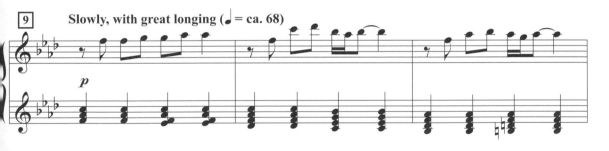

Light the ad - vent can - dles. Gath - er 'round the flame.

15

Warm your heart with prom - ise. Let your spir - it live a - gain.

17

mp

One by one, they flick - er, danc - ing in the night,

BARITONE *mp unis.*

One by one, they flick - er, flame in the

17

mp

19

chas - ing ev - 'ry shad - ow 'til the com - ing of the light.

night,_____ the com - ing of the light.

19

Come now, Mes-si-ah, set us free. Ve - ni,

ve - ni. Come now, Mes-si-ah, set us free.

* Tune: NUN KOMM, DER HEIDEN HEILAND, *Geistliche Gesangbüchlein*, 1524
Words: attr. St. Ambrose, 340-397. tr. William M. Reynolds, 1812-1876

CANTICLES IN CANDLELIGHT - SAB

Make us, Lord, Your can - dles. Blaze in ev - 'ry heart.

Burn a - way the doubt, and kin - dle hope in ev - 'ry part.

Make us Lord, Your peo - ple, burn-ing with Your light,

Make us Lord, Your peo - ple. Burn with Your

shin - ing in the shad - ows like a bea - con in the

light; a bea - con in the

night. The hope of heav - en for peace on earth,

night.

the gift of love,_____ great joy for all the world.

Our hearts are yearn - ing for Your re-turn - ing.

O come, Mes-si-ah, set us free. Ve - ni,

NARRATION:

From Luke's gospel, we hear this account:

God sent the angel Gabriel to Nazareth, a town in Galilee, to a young maiden named Mary. The angel said to her, "Greetings, you who are highly favored! The Lord is with you." Mary was greatly concerned with his words and pondered what kind of greeting this might be. But the angel gave comfort saying, "Do not be afraid, Mary; you have found favor with God. You will conceive and give birth to a Son, and you will call Him Jesus, for He shall save His people from their sins."

(Light the advent candle of Peace.)

COME, LONG-EXPECTED JESUS

(Congregational Anthem)*

Words by
CHARLES WESLEY (1707-1788)

Tune: **AUSTRIAN HYMN**
by FRANZ JOSEPH HAYDN (1732-1809)
Arranged by
JOSEPH M. MARTIN (BMI)

* Part for congregation is on page 107.

pect - ed Je - sus, born__ to set Thy peo - ple__ free.
to de - liv - er, born a Child, and yet a__ King;

From our fears and sins re - lease__ us. Let us find our
born to reign in us for - ev - er, now Thy gra - cious

rest in__ Thee. Is - rael's Strength__ and__ Con - so - la - tion,__
king - dom__ bring. By Thine all__ e - ter - nal__ Spir - it,__

Hope of ___ all the earth, Thou art; dear De-sire of
rule in ___ all our hearts a - lone. By Thine all suf-

ev - 'ry na - tion, Joy of ___ ev - 'ry ___ long - ing ___ heart.
fi - cient mer - it, raise us ___ to ___ Thy ___ glo - rious ___ throne.

Praise with - out ceas - ing, glo - ry___ in Thy

Pray and praise Thee with - out ceas - ing, glo - ry___ in___ Thy___

per - fect love.

per - fect___ love.

Pray and praise Thee with - out ceas - ing, glo - ry____ in____ Thy____ per - fect____ love. Al - le - lu - ia! Al - le - lu - ia! Al - le - lu - ia! Al - le - lu - ia!____

NARRATION:

Hear this encouraging declaration from scripture:

For behold, darkness covers the earth; and deep shadows over the people of the world; but the Morningstar will arise upon you, and His glory will be seen shining through you. And nations shall come to the Light, and kings to the brightness of His rising.

(Light the advent candle of Joy.)

AWAKE! ARISE! REJOICE!

Words by
JOSEPH M. MARTIN (BMI)

Tune:
PUER NOBIS
Trier Manuscript, 15th Century
Original music and arrangement by
JOSEPH M. MARTIN (BMI)

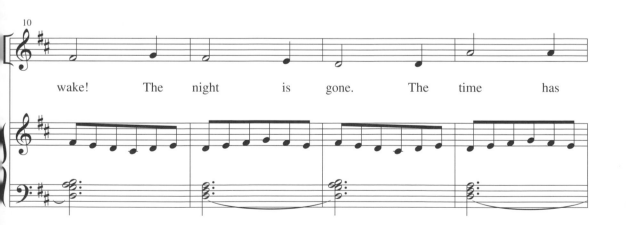

come ___ for joy - ful song; for in the

east a star ap - pears. The com - ing

of the Lord is near. ___

BARITONE

A - rise! A - rise and

greet the morn, for un - to us___ a
Child is born; and He will be a
might - y King, the Light of All, the
Prince of Peace.___

46

sealed in grace, in Beth - le - hem, ____ the

chos - en place._____

Al - le - lu - ia! Al - le - lu -

cresc. poco a poco

al - le - lu - ia!

with great celebration

with great celebration

wake! A - rise! Re - joice and sing. Let

mu - sic sound___ and prais - es ring.   Our

song   of   hope   is   now   re - stored.   De -

clare   the   com -   ing   of___

52

the_____ Lord!_____

Al - le - lu - ia!   Al - le -

lu - ia!   Sing a glad al - le - lu -

NARRATION:

This is how the birth of Jesus, the Promised One, came about:

Mary, His mother was pledged to be married to Joseph; but before they were together, she was found to be with Child through the Holy Spirit. Because Joseph was faithful to the law, and yet did not want to expose her to public disgrace, he had in mind to divorce her quietly. But after he considered this, a celestial messenger appeared to him and said, "Joseph, son of David, do not hesitate to take Mary as your wife. Her Child is from the Holy Spirit. She will give birth to a Son, and will call His name Jesus, for He will save His people from their sins." All this took place to fulfill what the Lord had said through the prophets, "A virgin shall conceive and give birth to a Son, and they shall call Him, Immanuel." (which means "God With Us")

(Light the advent candle of Love.)

CAROLS OF JOY AND HOPE

Arranged by
JOSEPH M. MARTIN (BMI)

Based on tunes:
JESU, JOY OF MAN'S DESIRING
GESÙ BAMBINO
TEMPUS ADEST FLORIDUM
SUSSEX CAROL
and "Pastorale" from *Christmas Concerto*

* Tune: JESU, JOY OF MAN'S DESIRING, from *Cantata 147*, Johann Sebastian Bach, 1685-1750
** Tune: GESÙ BAMBINO, Pietro A. Yon, 1886-1943
 Words: Pietro A. Yon, 1886-1943, tr. Frederick H. Martens, 1874-1932

night._____

BARITONE

was born_____ the Child,___ the Christ - mas Rose, the

King___ of Love___ and Light.

The

an - gels sang,___ the shep - herds sang, the grate - ful earth___ re-

re-

* Tune: "Pastorale" from *Christmas Concerto,* Arcangelo Corelli, 1653-1713
** Tune: TEMPUS ADEST FLORIDUM, A Spring Carol, 14th Century
Words: Joseph Simpson Cook, 1859-1933

CANTICLES IN CANDLELIGHT - SAB

60

* Tune: SUSSEX CAROL, traditional English melody
Words: Joseph M. Martin

CANTICLES IN CANDLELIGHT - SAB

Sing of thy won - drous Sav - ior's birth.

Slowly and swaying, like a lullaby (♩. = ca. 44)

FEMALE SOLO *with great gentleness*   *p*

Ah

BARITONE

hushed   *p*

Gen - tle Ma - ry

Slowly and swaying, like a lullaby (♩. = ca. 44)

NARRATION:

From Isaiah we receive this word:

How beautiful upon the mountain are the feet of those who bring good tidings; those who proclaim peace, all those who declare unto Zion, the Lord God Reigns. Break forth into joy! Sing together; for God has redeemed us, and now all the earth will behold the salvation of our God.

(Light the Christ candle.)

JOY TO THE WORLD

(Congregational Anthem)*

Words by
ISAAC WATTS (1674-1748)

Tune: **ANTIOCH**
by GEORGE FREDERICK HANDEL (1685-1759)
Arranged by
JOSEPH M. MARTIN (BMI)

* Part for congregation is on page 108.
** Tune from "Judas Maccabaeus," George Frederick Handel, 1685-1759

* Lyrics for stanzas 2 and 3 are echoed in a similar fashion.

CANTICLES IN CANDLELIGHT - SAB

68

heav'n,____ and heav'n,_____ and na - ture____ sing.
peat,____ re - peat,_____ the sound - ing____ joy.
as,____ far as,_____ the curse is____ found.

sing, and heav'n, and na - ture sing.

NARRATION:

Luke tells us of an amazing event surrounding the birth of Jesus:

Not far from Bethlehem, there were shepherds living out in the fields, keeping watch over their flocks by night. Suddenly, an angel appeared to them, and they were terrified. The angel said to them, "Do not be afraid for I bring joyful news for all people. This day in the city of David a Son is born to you. He is the Redeemer you have long awaited. You will find the Child wrapped in swaddling clothes and lying in a manger." Suddenly, the skies were filled with angelic beings, praising God and declaring, "Glory to God in the highest, and on earth, peace and goodwill to all."

When the angels had left them and gone to heaven, the shepherds said one to another, "Let us go to Bethlehem and see this wondrous miracle that has been revealed to us."

(Light the candle of Adoration and Worship.)

A CHRISTMAS MADRIGAL

Words by
J. PAUL WILLIAMS (ASCAP)

Music by
JON PAIGE (BMI)
Adapted by
JOSEPH M. MARTIN (BMI)

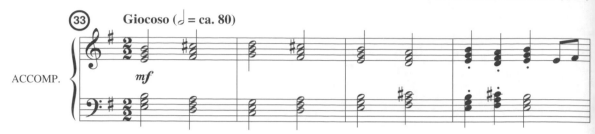

74

ho - di - e! Sing ho - san - na.

Gau - de - a - mus ho - di - e.

Hear the __ moun - tains __ ech - o - ing.

Christ-mas peo - ple, share the song. Let __ ju - bi - la - tion start.

Let the news of Je - sus' birth re - sound in ev - 'ry heart. No -

el! No - el! Re - joice and sing no - el! No - el!

No - el! No - el! Sing no - el! No - el!

Sing ho - san - na. Gau - de - a - mus

80

NARRATION:

Consider this scene from the gospel of Matthew:

After Jesus was born in Judea, Magi from the East came seeking the One who was born King of the Jews. They had seen His star arise in the night sky; and being scholars in prophecy, they realized this was a sign of great significance. With great joy, they followed the star till it came to rest over the place where the Child lived. They entered the house, and saw the Child with His mother Mary, and bowed down in humble adoration. With deep devotion and profound reverence, they presented Him with precious gifts and treasures, including gold, frankincense and myrrh. Even more, they brought hearts, filled with worship and praise.

(Light the candle of Faith.)

For the Chancel Choir of First United Methodist Church, Uvalde, Texas;
Susan Lovelace-Gerrish, Director of Music

TURN YOUR HEART TO CHRISTMAS

Words by
JOSEPH M. MARTIN (BMI)

Tunes: **CRANHAM**
by GUSTAV HOLST (1874-1934)
SHEEP MAY SAFELY GRAZE
by JOHANN SEBASTIAN BACH (1685-1750)
Arranged by
JOSEPH M. MARTIN (BMI)

Gen - tle hope em - brace you. Find the prom - ised Light. Give your-self to wor - ship. Reach for things a - bove. Turn your heart to Christ - mas. Know that you are loved.

(end solo)

84

In the still-ness of this night, as the an-gels sing, make your heart a man-ger for the new-born King.

Hold the gift of grace.

NARRATION:

Hear the word of the Lord:

I will make you as a light for the nations; that my salvation may reach to the end of the earth.

Arise and shine for your Light has come. The glory of the Lord has shone upon you.

For you once walked in darkness, but now you are walking in the Light of the Lord.

You are the light of the world. Let your light shine before everyone and reflect the glory of your heavenly Father.

Live as children of Light!

(Light the remaining candles to symbolize the sharing of the good news!)

A FESTIVE CHRISTMAS FLOURISH

(Congregational Anthem)*

Incorporating:
"The First Noel"
"It Came upon the Midnight Clear"
"Hark! The Herald Angels Sing"
Arranged by
JOSEPH M. MARTIN (BMI)

* Part for congregation is on pages 109-111.
** Tune: THE FIRST NOEL, traditional English melody
  Words: traditional English carol

92

night___ that was___ so deep. No - el,___ No -

el, No - el,___ No - el,___ born is the

King___ of Is - ra - el.

* Tune: CAROL, Richard Storrs Willis, 1819-1900
Words: Edmund H. Sears, 1810-1876

CANTICLES IN CANDLELIGHT - SAB

81 More quickly, with confidence (♩ = ca. 102)

89 CHOIR and CONGREGATION

S. *mf* unis. *

A.

Hark! the her - ald an - gels sing, __ "Glo - ry to the new - born King;

B. *mf*

89

* Tune: MENDELSSOHN, Felix Mendelssohn, 1809-1847
Words: Charles Wesley, 1707-1788

CANTICLES IN CANDLELIGHT - SAB

hosts pro-claim, "Christ is__ born in Beth - le - hem!" Hark! the her - ald

an - gels sing, "Glo - ry__ to the new - born King."

100

Optional Ending

(For those churches desiring a quiet, reflective ending, encircle the congregation for a final community singing of "Silent Night, Holy Night." Gradually light the candles of the congregation, until the auditorium is bathed in candlelight. Please feel free to adapt this moment to your church's own tradition.)

SILENT NIGHT, HOLY NIGHT

(Congregational Anthem)*

Words by
JOSEPH MOHR (1792-1848)
Translation by
JOHN FREEMAN YOUNG (1820-1885)

Tune: **STILLE NACHT**
by FRANZ GRÜBER (1787-1863)
Arranged by
JOSEPH M. MARTIN (BMI)

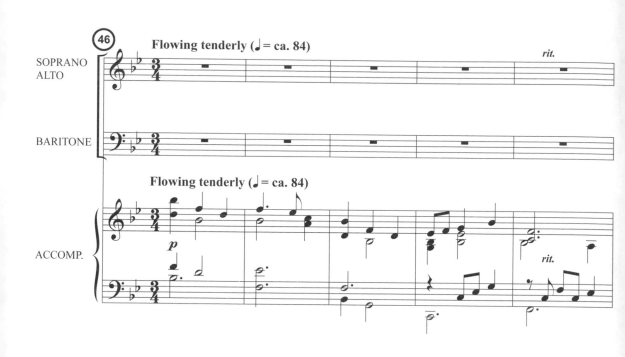

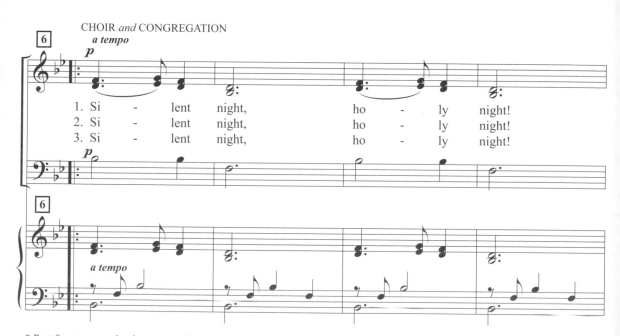

1. Si - lent night, ho - ly night!
2. Si - lent night, ho - ly night!
3. Si - lent night, ho - ly night!

* Part for congregation is on page 112.

sleep in heav - en - ly peace,
Christ the Sav - ior is born!
Je - sus, Lord, at Thy birth!

sleep in heav - en - ly peace.
Christ the Sav - ior is born!"
Je - sus, Lord, at Thy

birth!

dim. poco a poco

COME, LONG-EXPECTED JESUS

Words by
CHARLES WESLEY (1707-1788)

Tune: **AUSTRIAN HYMN**
by FRANZ JOSEPH HAYDN (1732-1809)
Arranged by
JOSEPH M. MARTIN (BMI)

CONGREGATION

unis. 1. Come, Thou long-ex-pect-ed Je-sus, born to set Thy peo-ple free.
parts 2. Born Thy peo-ple to de-liv-er, born a Child, and yet a King;
unis. 3. Come, Al-might-y to de-liv-er, let us all Thy grace re-ceive.

From our fears and sins re-lease us. Let us find our rest in Thee.
born to reign in us for-ev-er, now Thy gra-cious king-dom bring.
Sud-den-ly re-turn and nev-er, nev-er more Thy tem-ples leave.

Is-rael's Strength and Con-so-la-tion, Hope of all the earth, Thou art;
By Thine all e-ter-nal Spir-it, rule in all our hearts a-lone.
Thee we would be al-ways bless-ing, serve Thee as Thy hosts a-bove.

dear De-sire of ev-'ry na-tion, Joy of ev-'ry long-ing heart.
By Thine all suf-fi-cient mer-it, raise us to Thy glo-rious throne.
Pray and praise Thee with-out ceas-ing, glo-ry in Thy per-fect love.

CANTICLES IN CANDLELIGHT - SAB

JOY TO THE WORLD

Words by
ISAAC WATTS (1674-1748)

Tune: **ANTIOCH**
by GEORGE FREDERICK HANDEL (1685-1759)
Arranged by
JOSEPH M. MARTIN (BMI)

CONGREGATION

1. Joy to the world! The Lord is come! Let earth re-ceive her King.
2. Joy to the earth! The Sa-vior reigns! Let men their songs em-ploy;
3. No more let sins and sor-rows grow, nor thorns in-fest the ground.
4. He rules the world with truth and grace, and makes the na-tions prove

Let ev'-ry heart pre-pare Him room, and heav'n and na-ture sing, and
while fields and floods, rocks, hills and plains re-peat the sound-ing joy, re-
He comes to make His bless-ings flow far as the curse is found, far
the glo-ries of His righ-teous-ness, and won-ders of His love, and

heav'n and na-ture sing, and
peat the sound-ing joy, re-
as the curse is found, far
won-ders of His love, and
(1.) and heav'n and na-ture sing, and

(1.) and heav'n and na-ture sing, and heav'n and na-ture

heav'n, and heav'n, and na-ture sing.
peat, re-peat, the sound-ing joy.
as, far as, the curse is found.
won-ders, won-ders of His love.

sing,

THE FIRST NOEL

Words:
Traditional English Carol

Tune: **THE FIRST NOEL**
Traditional English Melody
Arranged by
JOSEPH M. MARTIN (BMI)

(after st. 1,
go to next carol.)

IT CAME UPON THE MIDNIGHT CLEAR

Words by:
EDMUND H. SEARS (1810-1876)

Tune: **CAROL**
RICHARD STORRS WILLIS (1819-1900)
Arranged by
JOSEPH M. MARTIN (BMI)

CONGREGATION

It came up-on the mid-night clear, that glo-rious song of

old, from an-gels bend-ing near the earth to

touch their harps of gold: "Peace on the earth, good

will to all, from heav'n's all gra-cious King." The
(men,)

world in sol-emn still-ness lay, to hear the an-gels sing.

HARK! THE HERALD ANGELS SING

Words by:
CHARLES WESLEY (1707-1788)

Tune: **MENDELSSOHN**
FELIX MENDELSSOHN (1809-1847)
Arranged by
JOSEPH M. MARTIN (BMI)

SILENT NIGHT, HOLY NIGHT

Words by
JOSEPH MOHR (1792-1848)
Translation by
JOHN FREEMAN YOUNG (1820-1885)

Tune: **STILLE NACHT**
FRANZ GRÜBER (1787-1863)
Arranged by
JOSEPH M. MARTIN (BMI)

CONGREGATION

1. Si - lent night, ho - ly night! All is calm, all is bright round yon vir - gin moth - er and Child! Ho - ly In - fant, so ten - der and mild, sleep in heav - en - ly peace, sleep in heav - en - ly peace.

2. Si - lent night, ho - ly night! Shep - herds quake at the sight. Glo - ries stream from heav - en a - far. Heav'n - ly hosts sing: "Al - le - lu - ia! Christ the Sav - ior is born! Christ the Sav - ior is born!"

3. Si - lent night, ho - ly night! Son of God, love's pure light, ra - diant beams from Thy ho - ly face with the dawn of re - deem - ing grace, Je - sus, Lord, at Thy birth! Je - sus, Lord, at Thy birth!